CANADIAN PAINTERS

—

PHAIDON

CANADIAN PAINTERS

EDITED BY DONALD W. BUCHANAN.
ADVISORY COMMITTEE FOR THE SELECTION OF THE REPRODUCTIONS
MARTIN BALDWIN · CURATOR OF THE ART GALLERY OF TORONTO
A.Y.JACKSON, LL.D.
H.O.McCURRY · DIRECTOR OF THE NATIONAL GALLERY OF CANADA,
OTTAWA.

MCMXLV
PUBLISHED BY THE PHAIDON PRESS · OXFORD & LONDON

CANADIAN PAINTERS

FROM PAUL KANE TO THE GROUP OF SEVEN

LONDON : THE PHAIDON PRESS
NEW YORK : OXFORD UNIVERSITY PRESS

PUBLISHED BY THE PHAIDON PRESS LTD · 14 ST GILES · OXFORD · AND 41 MUSEUM ST · LONDON · WC1
PRINTED BY HARRISON & SONS LTD · ST. MARTIN'S LANE · LONDON · ENGLAND · PRINTERS TO H.M. THE KING

PREFACE

GEOGRAPHY as much as tradition has influenced Canadian art. This can be seen from the reproductions is this book, which cover the period from the nineteenth century to about 1930. Best remembered from pioneering days is CORNELIUS KRIEGHOFF (1815-1872). Endowed with a talent for anecdote and illustration, this wanderer from Europe depicted winter scenes in Quebec with a facility that was much admired. The artists who followed him in the next few decades tended on the other hand to be mainly men who had come from the United Kingdom or, if native born, were firmly tutored in either the English academic or Barbizon traditions. By the end of the nineteenth century the more experimental developments in French art had, however, begun to influence a few of the younger painters who had gone to Paris to study, such as JAMES WILSON MORRICE (1865-1924).

The nationalist awakening, when it finally came, proved to be a mingling of both native stimulus and new techniques. Beginning before 1914, it reached its culmination in the formation of THE GROUP OF SEVEN in 1920. The emphasis of these painters was on the decorative treatment of landscape. They found in those ragged areas of woodland, rock, and hidden lakes, which cover much of central and northern Canada, the inspiration for many of their most distinctive canvases. As their principal spokesman, A. Y. JACKSON, has explained, it was this choice of subject which helped to create their style.

The reproductions have been selected from each period, but the largest number have been chosen from the opening quarter of the twentieth century. Since 1930 various other tendencies have come equally to the fore in Canadian painting, and these will be dealt with in a second volume.

PIONEER PAINTERS

The adornment of the parish churches with gilded and coloured carvings in wood, the cultivation of a simple but adequate colonial architecture and the growth, in a community isolated from metropolitan life, of rural handicrafts made up the artistic heritage of the French régime in Canada. Painting was a more sophisticated art, less prone to flourish in a frontier colony. The ecclesiastical examples which are still preserved from the eighteenth century are not notable. Shortly after 1760, a certain François Malepart de Beaucourt, the son of a military engineer, was, however, doing some creditable portraits and figure studies in Quebec.

After his death early in the nineteenth century, no other painter of interest turned up along the St. Lawrence until the German adventurer, Cornelius Krieghoff, arrived in Montreal in the early forties. Krieghoff, whose birthplace is variously given as Düsseldorf, and Amsterdam, the son of a wall-paper manufacturer, had been given a good education, for he seems to have studied art both in German schools and in Rotterdam.

After wandering about Europe, he came in 1837 to New York, joined the United States army, and fought in the Seminole Indian wars; later, when his regiment was stationed near the Canadian border, he deserted, married a French Canadian girl, and moved to Montreal. He also resided for a while in the neighbouring town of Longueuil. His qualities as a gay dog and as a wine bibber soon made him popular among the more lively young bloods of the English population. When he moved to Quebec City in 1853 these proclivities became more marked; they are recorded in many a canvas of "Chez Jolifou", a much frequented roadside tavern. (See plate 4, "The Merrymakers".)

At this time the fashion for buying coloured engravings and lithographs of North American life and scenery, such as those published by Currier and Ives, was everywhere the rage, and Krieghoff took advantage of it. He is known to have made at least one business trip to London to sell his canvases to publishers; also prints from his pictures were made in Philadelphia. His formula for rendering snow and ice, with hard glossy detail, like a mirror, was in the academic Dutch tradition of the day. On the other hand, when it came to describing autumn foliage, or the intense red rose of northern sunsets, he showed himself to be less restricted. In fact, he put down those colours with uninhibited realism. The English garrison officers used to buy his small canvases for a few pounds, and send them home for Christmas presents, yet in England the authenticity of those sunsets was always doubted. His best works are pleasing enough depictions of what were the more picturesque elements in his surroundings. The ones of winter scenes are preferred, but a few he did of Indians against backgrounds of deep forests are also admired.

Another "pioneer" artist was Paul Kane, who painted in York, Upper Canada, now Toronto, during the middle years of the nineteenth century. Kane, brought as a child to Canada from Ireland by his parents, had nursed from boyhood a desire to do a series of illustrations of North American Indians. "I had been accustomed," he wrote later, "to see hundreds of Indians about my native village." In 1841, when he was twenty-nine, he succeeded in visiting Europe, where he studied and made copies in the museums. In 1844, he returned to Canada and at once started to paint Indian encampments on Lake Huron. His great opportunity, however, came two years later, when the Hudson's Bay Company gave him authority to accompany their fur brigades across the Great Lakes and along the rivers of the western plains to Fort Edmonton. This was, perhaps, the most arduous sketching trip which any artist has ever made. It took three years, including most of twelve months devoted to voyaging by canoes from Fort Edmonton through the Rocky Mountains to the Pacific Coast and back. The country he covered was uninhabited except for roving bands of Indians, and a few white traders. The canvases which he did later from the sketches are brownish in colour, the drawing is perfunctory; but yet his paintings remain anthropological and historical documents of importance. His book, "Wanderings of An Artist among the Indians of North America", is well known and is considered a valuable travel narrative about the early North West.

THE PASTORAL LANDSCAPE

In the last quarter of the nineteenth century, the wealthy citizens of the new Dominion, adopting derivative modes of taste, began to buy imported canvases by Dutch and Barbizon artists as decorations for their prosperous, late Victorian mansions in Toronto and Montreal.

On the other hand, a few local painters of talent managed, despite these difficulties, to keep to the fore, and to sell their works. Most important among them were Homer Watson (1855-1936) and Horatio Walker (1858-1938). Both aimed, as Watson said, "to make pictures of attractive moods of nature." Of the two, Walker, however, paid more attention to rural genre, and his descriptions of every aspect of farm life on the Ile d'Orleans, where he lived, near the city of Quebec, are well known and through them he attained great popularity, particularly in the United States.

The work of Watson was closely connected with the landscape of the Grand River valley in western Ontario. He was born in the village of Doon, and there much of his best painting was done. Like Walker, he claimed to have been largely self-taught. As a boy he began to draw with a certain competence acquired by copying from the illustrations by Doré for "The Lives of the Martyrs". His later knowledge of technique, with its resemblance to Daubigny and Rousseau, was picked up afterwards, partly by travel and partly by association with artists in England.

His painting passed through several periods, from his early meticulous style to a broader, more solid naturalism, then in the last ten years of his career, he tried to work more directly in colour. In sentiment he was pantheistic. He set out, he declared, to create in pigment a composition capable of expressing the force and reality of that communion of the human and universal which he felt lurked continually behind the changing moods of nature, of the trees and skies of his native valley. In his old age, while he expressed some interest in the new Canadian movement in painting, he yet showed no desire himself to depict the northland. The cultivated, peaceful farmsteads of Ontario spelt reality to him ; they were, he wrote to a friend in 1929, " as much Canadian as jack pine and muskeg." He died on May 30, 1930, and visitors who travel by a side road from the city of Galt, Ontario, may visit the small museum in Doon that is kept to his memory.

The pastoral landscape was, of course, described by other artists, some of whom were excellent teachers, tolerant of experiment in others, and for that reason much respected by the generation which followed. There was, for example, William Brymner (1855-1925) in Montreal. He had come to Canada as a child, had studied later in France, and had been influenced by that cult of veiled simplicity of pattern based on Whistler. There exists, by one of his students, a good caricature of him pointing out the beauties of a Japanese print to a less appreciative friend. At the same time, he kept in touch with his surroundings in Quebec and painted many portraits and figure studies of rural types, as well as of more conventional subjects. There is perhaps a fresher approach to nature in the landscapes he did after 1900.

To all the young men in Montreal he was of great help, and, as headmaster of the Montreal Art School, he stood out for the more advanced work of his friends, Maurice Cullen and James Wilson Morrice.

JAMES WILSON MORRICE (1865-1924)

Morrice, for long known abroad as Canada's most distinguished painter, was a Montrealer born. Brought up in the Presbyterian atmosphere of a wealthy Scottish family of textile merchants, he at first departed little from their conventional norm. Then, however, when he was twenty-five, he deserted law school, and set off to study art in Paris. Once there his only formal master seems to have been Henri Harpignies, but he was soon influenced by many of the more modern schools of painters. His reputation abroad grew rapidly. In 1909, the critic, Louis Vauxcelles, wrote : " Since the death of James MacNeill Whistler, J. W. Morrice is unquestionably the American painter who has achieved in France and in Paris

(where he participates regularly in all the important exhibitions) the most notable and well merited place in the world of art." Yet, while Morrice adopted France as his second home, his background was and always continued to be North American. From year to year Montreal saw him return, mostly for short visits in the winter, when he went sketching along the St. Lawrence. He also contributed to exhibitions in the Dominion, and was made a member of the Royal Canadian Academy.

As for national sentiment, one need only look at his picture of "The Ferry, Quebec", now in the collection of the National Gallery of Canada, or that other scene of " Dufferin Terrace, Quebec", to realize that he was close to his best when painting his native land in its winter garb. On the other hand, he was equally fine in those last free creations of his brush, those canvases of the West Indies, done towards the end of his life. Each artist finds his stimulus in his own way ; and Morrice, it is safe to say, found his mostly by travelling. He was forever wandering from Paris to Morocco, from Venice to Montreal, and thence from Cuba to Trinidad.

His work went through many variations in style, he came close to imitation, once or twice, of experiments in the manner of, first Whistler and Conder, then much later, Matisse. Yet there was always something in every painting of his that was very much his own. Some French critics said that by setting his figures, like solid immovable counters in the landscape, he was able to induce an atmosphere of tender melancholy, which sentiment in his paintings they called Anglo-Saxon. Certainly a " divinest Melancholy ", in the sense of Milton's poem, is present in much of his work.

The French also commented upon his oily and rich pigments, and particularly the way in which he diffused throughout his canvases a gentle, at times almost imperceptible, pinkish glow. This appeared whether the pigment was laid on thickly, as in his early scenes of the Paris quays, or thinly as in later paintings of Montreal houses.

Morrice discovered and began to use this rose-colouring, which is so peculiar and so natural to the otherwise sombre darkness of a Canadian winter sky, when doing his first large canvases of Quebec scenery—that was back in the nineties—and he never seemed to forget its beauty. It is hardly an exaggeration to say that he afterwards painted Parisian skies with Canadian eyes. As a critic once wrote in the *Gazette des Beaux-Arts,* " There is much charm in the landscapes of James Wilson Morrice. Among the grey clouds covering his skies he scatters a rose of exquisite delicacy that he was the first to employ." That was Paris, the year 1911. At about this time most of his academic colleagues in Canada were still looking at Quebec and Ontario landscapes as if they were overcast with the pearly clouds of Dordrecht. No wonder Morrice wrote in 1910 to Newton MacTavish, in Toronto, " As you say, these English dealers with their pale Dutch monochromes have poisoned everything. Healthy, lusty colour, which you see in Canada, is no doubt considered vulgar." The contrast does not need to be underlined. The feeling which Morrice had for Canadian landscape, particularly winter atmosphere, was true.

Krieghoff, of course, had already depicted the life of these old settled parishes along the St. Lawrence, but Morrice recorded their appearance with a new charm and a whimsical simplicity. The small sleighs of the French Canadian farmers against a background of white and purplish snow always stood out as touches of humanity in his Quebec paintings. These sleighs have since been used as similar motifs by others ; they appear for example continually in the landscapes of A. H. Robinson, Clarence Gagnon, and A. Y. Jackson.

The sure facility which Morrice possessed for handling the more subtle values of colour in landscape, coupled with his organic sense of surface pattern, gives him a special eminence. His friend, Henri Matisse, with whom he spent the winters of 1911 and 1912 in Tangiers, was afterwards to describe his work as being full of delicate vision and touching tenderness in the depiction of closely allied values. His small sketches on wooden panels were always exquisite. His larger compositions on canvas, which he did usually in his studio on the Quai des Grands Augustins, in Paris, were, however, sometimes variable in quality. Nevertheless, the best of them are minor masterpieces, entitled to be ranked along with those of Sickert in England, of Bonnard and Vuillard in France, of Maurice Prendergast in the United States—artists who adopted and modified the colour harmonies of the impressionists and turned them into a more personal, more intimate, mode of painting.

As for his sketches, he worked on them as he sat at café tables in Tangiers and Havana, or on the terrace at Quebec, and the creation of them became, as time went on, a daily ritual. They seemed, as Clive Bell has remarked, to have been in the nature of a spiritual solace or to use a term that is found in one of Morrice's own notebooks, they were to him " un état d'âme ".

What kept Morrice slightly apart from some of the more advanced theorists among his friends abroad was his appreciation of what he often called " the more lenient artists ". In this way he, at an early stage in his career, came to admire Charles Conder, who was then known particularly for his sensitive paintings on silken fans. These two men, for a few years at the turn of the century, were often together in Paris. It is interesting to reflect now upon their similarity of character. Both placed equal emphasis upon the fleeting stimulants and beauties of existence, and both possessed the same devil-may-care attitude towards the politics of mankind.

SOME PAINTERS OF QUEBEC

In point of time, Maurice Cullen, who returned to Montreal from Paris in 1896, was the pioneer in Canada of impressionism. Along with his friend, Morrice, he helped introduce new and more atmospheric colours into Canadian painting. Yet there were noticeable differences between the two men. Cullen never could have looked at a trunk of a tree that he knew to be brownish red, and then have changed it on canvas to pure green or sheer purple in order to obtain a more suggestive and personal pattern. But Morrice could and did. Yet Morrice always admired his friend's honesty before nature. As he wrote in 1910, " Cullen, I see from the Montreal papers, has painted a good picture of St. John's, Newfoundland. He is the man in Canada who gets at the guts of things." They often worked together, usually on the Ile d'Orleans, where they visited Charles Porteous, on whose estate " Les Groisardières ", there are still murals by Cullen and also by Brymner, but Cullen's art was too delicate for the broad sweep of decorative panels.

He had come at an early age from Newfoundland to Montreal with his parents. There, as a young man, he had tried his hand at sculpture, then had changed to painting and had gone in 1889, at the age of twenty-three, to Paris to study at the Beaux-Arts. Upon his return to Montreal, he had to struggle along in relative hardship for many years. Yet he stuck to his vocation without taking up commercial art, or without recourse to pot-boiling. The grind was stern and long, there were days of poverty, but eventually, with the aid of a guarantee from a dealer, he managed to achieve a measure of comfort in his later years.

Interested in every aspect of the winter sun as it fell on snow and ice, or of light filtering through an overclouded sky, he recorded the atmosphere of his native province in all its changing moods. " Montreal with its old buildings, its ranks of cabs awaiting fares, the garnering of the ice harvest, streets with lighted windows of shops and moving traffic seen through the blizzard, proved congenial subjects with plenty of tonal

I

JAMES WILSON MORRICE : THE FERRY, QUEBEC.
NATIONAL GALLERY, OTTAWA

problems to solve," St. George Burgoyne wrote of him. Also, while these works presented difficulties enough, "the painter hunted something harder to interpret—vapour rising from open water in sub-zero weather." The result of such studies can be seen in the canvas "Ice Harvest". (Plate 16.)

He was, indeed, among that small but authentic band of true open-air painters who "seem to have thought nothing of anchoring their easels in deep snow and working in an Arctic gale." To him snow was not white, but all colours from pink and mauve to blue and green. Only he preferred the colder tones, and his paintings towards the end were generally of harsher scenes, of isolated lakes and rivers in the Laurentian hills.

Two other painters, Gagnon and Suzor-Côté, after 1907, were also to become closely associated in their work with the landscape of Quebec.

Clarence Gagnon (1880-1942), who came from the village of Ste. Rose, near Montreal, first took art classes under Brymner. Then in 1904, when he was twenty-five, he set out to study at the Académie Julian in Paris. Already, by 1906, he had achieved recognition in France, particularly for his etchings. After 1909, he returned to Canada where he sketched in the winter, mainly in the old town of Baie St. Paul, which lies isolated among the Laurentian hills on the north shore of the St. Lawrence. His earlier style in oils was subdued, and Whistlerian in simplicity. Later he moved towards a more rigidly patterned arrangement of brightly coloured cottages, sleighs, glistening hills and ice-bound rivers. Technical problems of pigmentation, after 1915, absorbed him more and more. Afterwards, in Paris, he did some celebrated work as an illustrator, particularly for collectors' editions of "Le Grand Silence Blanc" and "Maria Chapdelaine". After many years of absence in France, and in Norway and Sweden, he returned in 1936 to spend the last years of his life in Montreal.

While Gagnon came from a family that had urban connections, Marc Aurèle de Foy Suzor-Côté, who died in 1937, was completely a son of rural Quebec. Like the great French Canadian statesman, Sir Wilfred Laurier, his name is intimately connected with the small town of Arthabaska. Here his father was a notary, and here Marc Aurèle was born in 1864. His early studies and surroundings in the arts were purely ecclesiastical. When twenty years of age, that was in 1889, he helped decorate the walls of the parish church, and of the chapel in the local College du Sacré Coeur. In 1890, he went to France to study at the Beaux-Arts and at the Académie Julian, and for seventeen years he remained abroad. Finally, in 1907 he returned. The rest of his active career was divided between painting and sketching near Arthabaska in the summer and at other seasons in his studio in Montreal.

His work went through various phases of development. His small sculptures of "habitant" life are perhaps as well known as his paintings. The best of his canvases are done in a neatly impressionist technique, and their subjects range from Montreal street scenes to portraits of sturdy French-Canadian farmers.

J. E. H. MACDONALD (1873-1932)

J. E. H. MacDonald has been described as a "red-headed man, with a slightly dour, slightly shy, manner and a deep sense of humour." His career, like the occasional verse he wrote, was simple and sturdily homespun in pattern.

Along with Tom Thomson, he is probably the most indigenous painter whom Canada has yet produced. Yet, as an artist, he was forced, because of lack of patronage in Toronto, to spend much of his life in the tedious business of commercial design and in teaching. Only for a few brief years, from 1913 to 1929, was he able to devote himself more completely to painting. Yet he managed then, and afterwards on holidays, to produce some excellent canvases, and numerous oil sketches, remarkable for their vibrant singing quality of colour.

He had been born in Durham, England, of Canadian parents, and had come with them to Ontario in 1887, when he was fourteen. He had then had three years at art school in Hamilton, Ontario, followed by apprenticeship to a firm of lithographers in Toronto. His artistic development in the years immediately following was related mainly to the sketches he did of the beech and pine woods near his home in suburban Toronto, although at some early stage, perhaps in 1904, when he took a position for three years with a commercial art studio in London, England, he may have been influenced by the prevailing cult for Barbizon landscapes. Yet his first canvases, when placed on exhibition in Canada about 1908, showed little or no hint of European modes.

By his unaffected painting, by his interest in every aspect of rural scenery in Ontario, and by his passion for doing oil sketches directly from nature, he quickly impressed his associates at the Art and Letters Club in Toronto which he joined in 1911. Public recognition came the same year when a group of his sketches were shown there. Charles W. Jefferys wrote then as follows: " Mr. MacDonald's art is native—as native as the rocks, or the snow, or pine trees, or the lumber drives that are so largely his themes. He seems to be able to forget what other men have selected, and how other men have expressed themselves, and in an age of such universal information as ours, and a country so provincial and imitative in its tastes as Canada, these are rare qualities." Jefferys, who wrote this, had been an illustrator of competence in New York. Later he had returned to Toronto, and by 1905 he had begun to paint various compositions, clear and simple, of western prairies.

About 1912 MacDonald became friendly with Lawren Harris, of Toronto, who had studied art in Berlin; a year later he also met A. Y. Jackson, of Montreal, who had been at the Académie Julian, in Paris. Along with Arthur Lismer and F. H. Varley, painters from Yorkshire who had settled in Ontario, these artists formed, as early as 1913, the nucleus of that Canadian movement in painting which was to grow into the Group of Seven.

The stimulus of these associations played their part in the further development of MacDonald's career. Yet his lyrical appreciation of nature, and his new opportunities for travel in the great forests and lakes of northern Ontario, were of equal importance. There was also Scandinavian art, related to impressionism, but with a broader, bolder treatment of landscape. Examples of this he saw at an exhibition in Buffalo in 1913. What other indirect influences upon him there were few can have known, for he rarely talked or wrote about art, only about nature. On his frequent visits to Algoma he sent back letters that are deeply expressive of the awe he felt before those stupendous panoramas of craggy hills, of mixed coniferous and hardwood forests. These sketching trips provided him with many memorable impressions. As he wrote of the Montreal river, where he did the sketches for his large canvas, "The Solemn Land," in 1918: "Looking at it from the railway track on our way home, we felt we could understand something of the feeling of the early Canadian explorers. The whole scene seemed so primeval and unspoiled, and the great broad river another St. Lawrence waiting for discoverers."

By 1921 and 1922, MacDonald was producing his best work, the most satisfyingly composed and the most brilliant in colouring. In "Gleams on the Hills" (Plate 32) he uses curving strokes of pure pigment to consolidate his pattern. Then there is "A Northern Hilltop," also of Algoma, but repainted in 1931 (Plate 36).

Struggles to earn a living by easel painting did not prove successful, so he gladly took the teaching position offered him in 1921 at the Ontario College of Art. He became an instructor of design and applied art, and later principal of the college. On his holidays in those last years of his life, he went mainly to the Rocky Mountains. Their great solitudes seemed to satisfy that continual craving which he possessed for quietness and meditation among the untouched scenes of wild nature. He would go climbing high into the glacier lined passes round Lake O'Hara in Yoho Park, British Columbia, where he used to camp in a rented cabin, and sit there all afternoon on some scree slope and sketch, with no noise round him save the occasional sibilant call of a marmot among the rocks. He now changed his style, but the experiments which he began to make in simplification of pattern were not felicitous. Some of his larger alpine compositions became as flat as any poster, although a few of the smaller ones still retained something of his former freedom.

His duties at the College of Art were strenuous. He had little or no time after 1928 for working on studio canvases. In fact, he was exhausted by his teaching tasks, and the physical collapse which resulted brought on his death in November, 1932.

In retrospect one can say of his painting, with the exception of that mountain interlude, that " his ideal was to portray the forest ". That ambition he honourably achieved.

TOM THOMSON (1877-1917)

When his friends erected the cairn at Canoe Lake in honour of his memory, they called him " Tom Thomson, artist, woodsman and guide . . . who lived humbly but passionately with the wild ".

Born in Ontario in 1877, Thomson came of pioneer farming stock. His parents' home, near Owen Sound on Lake Huron, had its site in a rolling countryside, of pleasant fields crossed with old rail fences, with patches of elms and birches and pines on the higher hills; there he had, as a boy, wandered along the streams and woodland slopes and learned the ways of camping. Also he had been musical; in his family, as a neighbour relates, " they were all music minded ".

His first job had been as an apprentice in a machine shop. Then he had been to business school, and finally, in 1901, when he was twenty-four, he had gone west to the Pacific Coast of the United States, to Seattle, where he had learned the trade of photo-engraving. He returned to Ontario in 1905, and about 1910 joined Grip

Limited, a firm of commercial designers in Toronto. There his fellow employees used to go sketching together on Sundays along nearby ravines and rivers or to more distant lakes on week-ends, and they took Thomson along; he would do a few small oil panels and then, in between, play his mandolin.

Through his friendship with J. E. H. Mac-Donald, then head designer at Grip Limited, Thomson no doubt was encouraged to turn his new-found hobby of sketching in oils (he had done a few water-colours before in Seattle) into more profound channels. But an event that helped perhaps equally to change the course of his career was a canoe trip he took in 1912, through a relatively untouched area of northern Ontario. First, that summer he had spent a short time in Algonquin Park, a government reserve of thousands of lakes and countless streams, and then later, with a friend, Broadbent, he had set out on a two months' camping tour of the less frequented Mississauga Forest Reserve. For eight weeks the two men travelled by canoe, down rivers and lakes that bore names which were both Indian and euphoneous, from Bisco-tasing to Audinadong. They fished, for from boyhood Thomson had been an excellent angler, and sometimes they painted. Then there were torrential rains, and the canoe was swamped. They ran rapids between deep gorges, and at the end of one stretch known as the " forty miles of white water ", the boat capsized and they had to wade into the stream to rescue some of their panels.

Few could forget such exploits; throughout the winter that followed Thomson kept talking about them, and he was ready and eager for the north again in the spring. But in the meantime, people were hearing about him, were becoming interested in his sketches. Dr. J. M. MacCallum, of Toronto, who was already a friend of MacDonald, and who knew the country the campers had been through, relates that he came that winter to 6, Wellesley Street, a rooming house where Thomson lived, to see the artist. Thomson, however, disclaimed any pretensions to being a painter; in conversation he was more enthusiastic about the geographical and piscatorial wonders of his journey, but, as Dr. MacCallum reports, " As I looked over his sketches, I realized their truthfulness, their feeling and sympathy with the grim fascinating northland."

Thus Thomson found the man who was to become his patron the following year, and was to buy enough of his oil panels to allow him to leave his routine job in Toronto so that he might spend many months in Algonquin Park.

That winter he had also done his first studio canvas. It was hung in the annual spring show of the Ontario Society of Artists, and to his astonishment awarded a prize. This picture, " A Northern Lake ", was fairly sombre, and bears little relationship to his later work.

His association now with the artist A. Y. Jackson was of some significance. Jackson, who came from Montreal, and who had been in Paris, possessed a thorough training in impressionism. The two men met, through Dr. MacCallum, and then, in January, 1914, in order to save money, they decided to take a studio together, which they kept until Jackson returned to Montreal a year later to enlist in the army.

Thomson's sketches at the beginning of this period were still murky, but by the end of 1914, as Jackson relates, " he was making amazing strides, his colour becoming richer, his composition freer and bolder."

Thomson had, of course, some previous apprenticeship in design. He had worked for over ten years in engraving plants, where his early training had been the drawing of designs for book covers and title pages. Those sprouting lines and vegetable curves which he had used in his commercial work were now transferred to more than a few of his canvases, although later he dropped these more fanciful touches for a more personal and more solidly hewn style.

His work passed through several stages, but little chronological demarcation is possible. The reason is that, at one time, he would be trying out the pointillist technique of small and tidy strokes of pure colour on his canvases, at another he would be letting his brush go into wider, firmer patches of pure colour. Yet his more characteristic style was the more vigorous one. In the canvas, " The Jack Pine ", done in 1916, there is a surface composition like tapestry. In this particular approach there is perhaps some crudity, but Thomson did not mean it for that. He was not trying to create a sensation by the suddenness of these flat patterns of tree and branches, he was rather trying to record in his own honest fashion the strength and clarity of the Algonquin landscape as he saw it. From his last and unfinished picture, " The West Wind ", one might believe that he was beginning in 1917 to concentrate a little on the softening of these harsher outlines.

Such speculation, however, is idle, for his death came suddenly by drowning in July, 1917. His ambition when he came north that spring had been to make sketches day by day of the unfolding year. During those last months he was absorbed completely in this task. He was busily recording each changing aspect of the landscape, as the last

II

JAMES E. H. MACDONALD: THE POTATO FIELD, ONTARIO.
COLLECTION OF THE RT. HON. VINCENT MASSEY, P.C., LONDON

snow departed, as the first spring buds appeared, then the coming of the early flowers, the rush of flood waters, and finally, the deepening green of foliage on the hardwood trees. Shortly after telling his friend, the ranger, Mark Robinson, that this achievement was completed, he disappeared. Later his canoe was found overturned on a lake, but his body did not come to the surface until some days later.

In appearance Tom Thomson was six foot two in height, largely built but graceful, with black hair and a finely shaped nose. He was known as an excellent companion, as a fisherman of great skill, as a guide of repute in the forest. In the north, when he required money, he would work gladly at whatever manual job might come his way, even if it were only the clearing away of underbrush for a camp site. His needs were, however, simple : food for himself, tubes of paint for his sketch box, and repairs for his canoe.

One must not, however, misunderstand the meaning of those last years of his in Algonquin Park. He was not, as legend would have it, some hermit of the wilds. He was rather a practising artist, who had to find a way of life for himself on a small income. He knew how much money he could earn from occasional commercial work in the winter, and from odd jobs such as a guide or handyman in the woods in the summer. So he chose a relatively direct and congenial method of accomplishing the purpose he had in mind. In this way he was still able to return for some four months a year to his small studio in Toronto, " Tom's shack " as it was called, to work on his large canvases.

What is most remarkable about him is this, that his painting, or the greatest part of it, was done in one comparatively small area of ragged, timbered country, which was not in any orthodox sense, either majestic or strikingly beautiful. Already, when he first came to Algonquin Park, its tall trees were being cut down, and the section which he frequented was also partly fire-swept and flooded by beaver ponds. He depicted every aspect of this region with realism and honesty in about two to three hundred small oil panels, most of which are brilliant in colour and straightforward in execution. He also did twenty or so canvases, in the course of his short career, most of which are now in public collections. As his friend Jackson wrote in tribute : " Not knowing all the rules and conventions regarding what is beautiful he found it all beautiful, muskegs, burnt trees, drowned land, log chutes, beaver dams, northern lights, the flight of wild geese."

THE GROUP OF SEVEN AND SOME RELATED PAINTERS (1907-1921)

Although the first exhibition of the Group of Seven was held only in 1920, the friendships and mutual interests of most of the men concerned had begun much earlier. To understand not only their background, but also that of certain related artists, it is necessary to go back to 1907, the year in which J. E. H. MacDonald returned to Toronto from his sojourn in England. Here then is a detailed chronological outline of the growth of a Canadian movement in painting. Of necessity, there is some repetition here of biographical details already mentioned on preceding pages, but such brief recapitulations, when they occur, serve their purpose in pointing out the more significant relationship between the artists involved.

1907-10 THE PROTAGONISTS

By 1907 MacDonald and Thomson are both working for engraving firms in Toronto. Most of the other artists who will meet them later and become their friends are that year visiting Europe or, like Varley, who is in England, and Lismer, who is in Antwerp, have yet to come to Canada. Jackson, after a period of hardship in Montreal, has earned enough money for travel abroad, and is at the Académie Julian in Paris. Having previously studied at this same school, J. W. Beatty, of Toronto, is indulging a romantic bent for painting in the Netherlands. A little younger than the others, Lawren Harris, who comes from a well-to-do family in Brantford, Ontario, has gone to Germany. He wanders about there and elsewhere on the Continent, sketches considerably and takes some tuition in art, mainly in Berlin.

In Toronto, MacDonald in the spring of the following year has his work shown for the first time at the annual exhibition of the Ontario Society of Artists. But more prominently displayed on the walls are paintings by Jefferys of western and prairie scenes, and one of a Quebec town by A. H. Robinson, of Hamilton, Ontario. These particular canvases provide tentative notes of a new but strictly naturalist approach to Canadian landscape.

In 1909, both Harris and Jackson come back to Canada, but Harris does not remain long, as he is commissioned by *Harper's Magazine* in New York to do a special series of illustrations on Arabia, and he departs for that country. Beatty, who only two years ago was proud of his paintings of Dutch scenes, now gains the distinction of being the first artist to go into the Canadian northland by canoe to sketch and paint.

MacDonald becomes, during 1910, the head designer for Grip Limited, in Toronto. This summer he goes on his first trip to Georgian Bay, where he is delighted with the open stretches of water, the pines and rugged islands. He stays at the cottage of Dr. MacCallum. Jackson also visits Georgian Bay, but at the moment he prefers to paint in the Quebec countryside, where, using a modified impressionist technique, he turns out some noticeably sober compositions.

Robinson has now moved to Montreal, and is able to concentrate on doing landscapes of Quebec. Cullen exhibits his canvas of St. John's, Newfoundland, and Jackson reports that Cullen, as well as Morrice, is now proving to be an influence on all the younger artists in Montreal.

Sometime later this year, Thomson joins Grip Limited and meets MacDonald.

1911-12 GRIP LIMITED

In 1911, several canvases by Harris are hung in the spring show of the Ontario Society of Artists; those of street scenes in Toronto, of simple homely buildings and roadways, attract attention. Lismer arriving in Canada from Sheffield, joins Grip Limited. A new apprentice there is twenty-one year old Frank Carmichael, who, up until now, has been working in his father's carriage shop in Orillia, Ontario. MacDonald, now thirty-seven, decides that to be a painter in one's spare time is not enough, so he leaves the firm to embark on a new and less commercial career. Along with Lismer he encourages Thomson to take up sketching out of doors as a hobby. The men from Grip Limited now go further afield on their Sunday sketching expeditions, to Lake Scugog, fifty miles away, where they paint between intervals of fishing and duck shooting.

MacDonald, in 1912, finishes his canvas " Tracks and Traffic ", and in this same year he is admitted to the Royal Canadian Academy; Thomson makes his initial trip to Algonquin Park. Later he goes on that remarkable canoe voyage of three hundred miles through the Mississauga Forest Reserve. Lismer revisits Sheffield and persuades his friend Varley, an excellent portrait painter, to come to Canada. Varley, to use his own words, has, after leaving the Royal Academy of Fine Arts in Antwerp, been spending " several years illustrating in London and several years drifting in the underworld." The newcomer also joins Grip Limited, then Thomson and Carmichael move to the firm of Rous and Mann, and Varley follows them. Lismer will later write of the painting they were doing at this time, " We were adventurous but it never got into our pictures." As for Jackson, he has been away from Canada; he has been travelling and painting in Italy.

1913-14 THE NORTH COUNTRY

The year 1913 becomes the key date in the formation of those enthusiasms for northern landscape which will later bring some of these painters together as the Group of Seven. Of the spring exhibition of the Ontario Society of Artists, one critic writes, " Of the ninety-one paintings exhibited, at least ten were distinctly of this country." By the ten he refers mainly to those of MacDonald, Harris, Thomson and Beatty. Hearing that Jackson has returned from Italy, Harris now gets in touch with him by letter in Marieville, Quebec, and his optimistic account of the development of a more nationalist type of painting in Toronto moves Jackson to reply, " It really looks as though the sacred fires were going to burst into flame by the faithful efforts of yourself and MacDonald." His picture " Edge of the Maple Wood ", is bought by Harris, and partly because of the money received from it, and partly because of a guarantee from Dr. MacCallum to buy enough of his work to cover expenses, Jackson is encouraged to remain in Canada instead of going to the United States, as he had planned to do. He now meets MacDonald and the others in Toronto.

This summer and autumn everyone goes sketching in the north. Lismer makes his first trip to Algonquin Park, where he camps for a few weeks with Thomson, who has left his job and is spending eight months of the year in the forest. Later, in Toronto, Jackson works in Harris' studio, where he completes his first experimental canvas, " Terre Sauvage ", the development of which is watched with great curiosity by the others. This same year he also finishes the noticeably decorative picture, " Night, Georgian Bay."

All these artists are now closely united in outlook and habits. Even Varley, who is essentially a portrait painter, goes on occasion to Georgian Bay to paint. Their work, nevertheless, is still, except for certain canvases by Jackson, mostly a straightforward naturalist rendering of landscape. Financed by Harris and by Dr. MacCallum, a commodious structure called the Studio Building is erected early in 1914 on Severn Street in Toronto. Into this most of them move. Late this summer Jackson and Beatty visit the Rocky Mountains, but Jackson, not especially relishing the great summits and glaciers, returns to spend the autumn " until the snow begins to fly " with Thomson in his Algonquin camp.

1915-17 THE WAR

In the second year of the war, 1915, jobs in the field of commercial art become more and more restricted, and paintings prove difficult to sell. The Ontario Society of Artists, however, holds an exhibition. Thomson shows a painting of a northern river which is bought by the National Gallery of Canada. Carmichael, recently returned from Europe, where he had been studying for a year in Antwerp, has his first canvas hung, a scene of the north, while Lismer has one of Georgian Bay, and MacDonald one of logs on the Gatineau river. Commenting on their work, a critic writes, " They have wakened up their elders." Jackson, having gone to Montreal in December, 1914, now enlists in June for overseas service. Thomson shares a studio with Carmichael for a while, but then moves off again to the north, where he is busy from spring thaw to autumn snowfall. On his return to Toronto in the winter, he takes to living in a small shack beside the Studio Building ; there Lismer sometimes comes to paint, too.

The year 1916 sees a controversy over " The Tangled Garden." This is a canvas by MacDonald, a routine enough description of flowers and shrubs, enlivened by touches of bright pigment. Yet it arouses newspaper criticism, and the artist obtains the reputation among the public of being a " radical " painter. Lismer later goes to Halifax, where he becomes the principal of the newly organized Nova Scotia College of Art.

In 1917, Thomson is beginning to be better known, but then, as he achieves recognition, he is mysteriously drowned in Canoe Lake. Beatty, who has long been one of his friends, helps to erect a cairn to his memory. As for MacDonald, he has not been at all prosperous, he gives up his house in Thornhill and moves to Toronto ; he falls ill and does not paint for months. Harris has been in the army, is now discharged, and begins to work with his palette again. A government project for Canadian war memorials is launched, and both Beatty and Varley are offered commissions as official artists. Jackson, after having served over two years as a private with the infantry, is withdrawn from field service and given a similar post, while in Halifax, Lismer is assigned the job of depicting harbour scenes, landscapes with shipping, which he does in a technique that is still impressionist in flavour but stronger in colour than before (see Plate 85).

1918-19 ALGOMA

This year, 1918, is notable as it marks the discovery of Algoma by MacDonald. That region is a more distant, a more rocky, and generally a country of more magnificent panoramas than Algonquin Park. The explorers there this autumn are MacDonald, F. H. Johnston (whom the others have known from their previous commercial associations at Grip Limited), Harris and their friend, Dr. MacCallum. The grandeur of this scenery, its powerful contrast of light and shade, has an immediate effect, but in different ways, on each of the painters. In MacDonald, there begins to develop that fluidity of colour and contour which marks the best of his work. Harris is attracted more by the deeply etched outlines of the north shore of Lake Superior.

By the next autumn the appeal of Algoma has spread. Jackson, having finished his work as an official war artist, accompanies MacDonald north on the " second box-car trip," so-called because they had to travel by work car on the regional railway which serves that remote district. This year Lismer returns from Halifax and takes a position at the Ontario College of Art. MacDonald exhibits " Leaves in the Brook."

Some of the war paintings have been displayed before the public in London, and the English critics have much to say in praise of Varley's scenes of the battlefields. (Plate 68.) Of them a writer on the *Daily Telegraph* states, " We find a massive objectivity, a sense of all-pervading tragedy."

1920-21 THE GROUP IS FORMED

The reunion of all these artists at the conclusion of the war brings a new solidarity into their efforts. They meet constantly in Toronto, and by the spring of 1920 are organizing a joint exhibition. In May, Carmichael, Harris, Jackson, Johnston, Lismer, MacDonald and Varley present

III
TOM THOMSON : THE ARTIST'S HUT.
THE NATIONAL GALLERY, OTTAWA

a show of their own. It is entitled " An Exhibition by a Group of Seven Painters ". The name sticks. Thus the " Group of Seven " is born. In the foreword to their catalogue they state their nationalist purpose, and add that they are " imbued with the idea that art must grow and flourish in a land before the country will be a real home for its people." Three others, including Robinson, participate in this exhibition by invitation.

The second Group show takes place in 1921, but Johnston is no longer among those contributing. Thirty of their pictures from the previous year are sent on a tour of various galleries in the United States. As if to counteract the attempt now being made by various critics to label them as a " school ", the artists declare in the introduction to their second catalogue, " We have no group formula and are conscious of widely divergent aims."

MacDonald this year paints two of his best known canvases, " The Solemn Land " and " Gleams on the Hills ", while Jackson begins to forsake northern Ontario for French Canada, where, following in the tradition that Krieghoff had begun and Morrice had developed, he creates the first of a long succession of snow and spring landscapes, which depict the farmsteads and cultivated hillsides of the lower St. Lawrence valley. His sketching companion this year is Robinson. As for Harris, he has already embarked on the more analytical of his Lake Superior canvases, and his work now attracts from the reviewers those startled comments which they had previously reserved for MacDonald.

AFTERMATH
(1922-1933)

Not everyone appreciated the boldness with which some of these artists portrayed the Canadian landscape. The National Gallery of Canada, however, quickly encouraged the new movement by purchasing various pictures by members of the Group. This is not the place for the story of the controversy which arose over that action ; let it be sufficient to say that the dispute waxed furious, and even reached the floor of the House of Commons in Ottawa. In the heat of the battle, some of the older painters accused the Group of violating nature, in return Harris wrote strongly in terms such as these, " It is blasphemy to wilt under the weight of ages ; to succumb to second-hand living ; to mumble old, dead, catch-phrases ; to praise far-off things and sneer at your neighbour's clumsiness."

From 1922 onwards Harris, MacDonald, Lismer and Jackson travelled widely throughout the Dominion. In fact, these artists set about with calculated thoroughness to describe every element of Canadian geography, from the fishing villages of Nova Scotia to the Rocky Mountains and the Arctic Ocean. Their efforts were rewarded by the praise with which critics in England and France received their works when shown at the Wembley Exhibition in 1924 and 1925, and in Paris in 1927.

In 1926, the addition of A. J. Casson, a Toronto artist who liked to depict the tidy frame architecture of Ontario villages, brought their number to seven again. They had been accused of neglecting figure painting, but this lack was partly made up by adding an eighth member, Edwin Holgate, in 1931. Like so many of the artists before him from Montreal, Holgate had studied first under William Brymner, and then at various academies in Paris. He is best known for his woodcuts of life in the rural parishes and lumber camps of Quebec, and for his sturdy portraits in oil of Canadian men and women of all classes and types. Sometimes he also does landscapes with figures. Representation from western Canada was obtained when L. L. FitzGerald, of Winnipeg, Manitoba, became a member in 1932. His work possesses all the sharp dryness of the air and skies of his native province, and his drawing a restraint and a refinement of line.

As can be seen, it is difficult to isolate the Group as a unit. Its members were individuals, and they each developed much in their own way.

Jackson, from his Algoma periods onwards, has employed a process of decorative simplification in which, however, his earlier subtleties of colour have remained. These are most noticeable in his rendering of distant fields of snow.

Compared to Jackson and MacDonald, Harris soon developed a more formalized approach to Canadian scenery. He was the most intellectual and philosophical of the Group, and his painting was in a sense a spiritual wrestling with chaotic nature. He set out to resolve the inarticulate disorder of the northern landscape by means of analysis. He isolated certain rock shapes, the sheath-like structure of a burnt pine, the elongated and graceful cylinder of the trunk of a birch tree. These forms he put together, " like sculpture ", in compositions which were possessed of a cold and simple dignity.

Varley, although he chose similar subjects at times, was never as analytical as the others. From his first work in portraiture, done when he emerged forty years ago from the Royal Academy of Fine Arts in Antwerp, to his latest sketches of Eskimo settlements in the Canadian Arctic, he has kept to a strain of personal lyricism. What

IV
ALEXANDER YOUNG JACKSON: ALGOMA LAKE.
COLLECTION OF H. O. McCURRY, Esq., OTTAWA

he, however, has gained from his experiences in Canada is colour. The more brownish tones which were in his English canvases disappeared soon after his arrival in Ontario. Since then he has always been the most luminous of the Seven in his handling of pigment, particularly in his greens, a colour which the others never saw in such varied lights. After 1926, he went to live and to teach for many years in Vancouver. Outside of his work as a portrait painter, he is most at home in some of his landscapes of British Columbia. This is especially true of his watercolours of the misty, moisture bedecked, mountains of the Pacific Coast.

In 1933 the Group of Seven came to an end as a separate entity. Its members had for some time wished to form a larger organization which would include others who were in sympathy with their aims. The new group, which came into being that year, was called the Canadian Group of Painters, and its first president was Jackson. In this society, their work came into the full blossoming of achievement. Yet there were other facets of Canadian life, other moods of art, to be treated still. Since 1933 more diverse impulses have begun to stimulate our painters. The description of these will be the concern of the second volume in this series.

THE CONTRIBUTION OF THE GROUP

The members of the Group of Seven made a bold frontal attack on the sterner aspects of Canadian geography. They forsook the peaceful farmlands, they went instead to the forest, and to that great rock shield which covers half of Canada. There in the north they travelled on their vacations, on holidays which took them back romantically through time to the pioneer days of roughing it in the bush. Much of the resulting appeal of their canvases was related to this nostalgia for nature. Also, Canadians after the war of 1914-18, were developing a full-fledged nationalism; they were proud of their open spaces and great hills and mountains. "We have a background of epic grandeur," said Arthur Lismer on a lecture tour he made of the Dominion, "and the modern movement here is a return to nature for sustenance."

By emphasizing shapes and contours in their canvases, artists like Jackson, Harris and Lismer made even the most casual spectator conscious of rock-girt lakes, towering mountains and clear horizons. These they proclaimed as symbols of Canadian sentiment. As Jackson explained, "We frankly abandoned our attempts at literal painting, and treated our subjects with the freedom of a decorative designer."

Of course, elsewhere, and particularly in France, there had been already, towards the turn of the century, a movement towards the use of colour to form sharply defined surface patterns. The artists who formed the Group of Seven, were aware of these tendencies in other countries. Also many neighbouring painters from the United States were adopting simplification of contour in their landscapes, particularly of New England winter scenes, and good or bad as their work may have been, it appears to have influenced the Canadians. Jackson, for example, wrote to Lawren Harris in 1913: "I feel pretty much as you do about American painting, healthy and vigorous much of it, and much of it slick and clever, but none of it profound. Still I feel we have a lot to learn from their out-of-door painters."

Yet the style, that most of the Group employed at the peak of their common purpose, that is immediately after 1920, was dictated not so much by outside influences as it was by that tumbled panorama of northern wilderness which they had set out to depict.

Describing his sketching in Algoma, Jackson said, "One must know the north country intimately to appreciate the great variety of its forms. . . . From sunlight in the hardwoods with bleached violet-white tree trunks against a blaze of red and orange, we wander into the denser spruce and pine woods where the sunlight filters through; gold and silver splashes playing with startling vividness on a birch trunk or patch of green moss. Such a subject would change entirely in ten minutes, and unless the first impression was firmly adhered to, the sketch would end in confusion."

Confronted by these variegated patches of uneven timber and foliage, of small bushes and rock lined lakes, Jackson and Lismer, in particular, soon found themselves unable effectively to use their former impressionist techniques. So they fell naturally into a more analytical approach. They simplified as much as possible, they eliminated as much as possible. The atmosphere, too, in the north was clear and bright, and the outlines of distant hills, and even of clouds, were sharp and distinct. These qualities also influenced them.

BIOGRAPHICAL NOTES AND LIST OF PLATES

PAUL KANE (1810–1871)

Paul Kane was born in Mallow, County Cork, Ireland, the son of Michael Kane. His family came to Canada in 1818 or 1819 and settled in Toronto, then called York. He was largely self-taught, although he travelled some and visited a few European museums before 1845. In the spring of 1846 he set out on a journey to the western plains, and his travels and adventures during the next few years in the North-West were varied and spectacular. The largest collection of his pictures is in the Royal Ontario Museum in Toronto.

PLATE 1 : *Kee-a-kee-ka-sa-coo-way (after 1850)* 30 × 25. *Royal Ontario Museum, Toronto.*

PLATE 2 : *Indian Encampment along the Islands of Lake Huron (probably 1845)* 18 × 29. *The Art Gallery of Toronto.*

CORNELIUS KRIEGHOFF (1815–1872)

Born in Dusseldorf, Germany. Studied at Rotterdam and afterwards travelled in Europe and America. Subsequently lived in Montreal and Quebec, where he painted French-Canadian scenes. A memorial exhibition of his work was held at the National Gallery, Ottawa, in 1934.

PLATE 3 : *Montmorency Falls in Winter (1853)* 36 × 48. (*In Krieghoff's time there was a famous ice cone here.*) *Col. George Cantlie, Montreal.*

PLATE 4 : *Merrymaking (1860)* 34½ × 48. *J. T. Ross, Esq., Quebec.*

PLATE 5 : *The Hunters (1858)* 14½ × 17½. *Dr. J. L. Robinson, Toronto.*

HOMER R. WATSON (1855–1936)

Born in Doon, Ontario. For the most part he was self-taught, although he was associated for some time with the painters, Sir George Clausen and E. J. Gregory, in England. He worked in his native village of Doon but visited England and the continent of Europe at intervals, the first time in 1887. He was elected R.C.A. in 1882.

PLATE 6 : *The Lone Cattle Shed (1894)* 18 × 24. *Mrs. N. W. Rowell, Toronto.*

PLATE 7 : *The Flood Gate (1900)* 32½ × 46¾. *The National Gallery of Canada, Ottawa.*

AURÈLE DE FOYE SUZOR-CÔTÉ, R.C.A. (1869–1937)

Born in Arthabaska, Quebec. Studied in Paris at the École des Beaux-Arts, and the Académies Julian and Colarossi. He returned to Canada in 1907. Elected R.C.A. 1914.

PLATE 8 : *Portrait of François Taillon (1921)* 27½ × 23¼. *Art Association of Montreal.*

FRANKLIN BROWNELL, R.C.A. (1856–   )

Born in New Bedford, Mass. Studied first at Boston Museum of Fine Arts, and later at the Académie Julian in Paris. Came to Canada in 1886 as headmaster of the Ottawa Art School. Elected to the Royal Canadian Academy, 1895. He painted during several seasons in the West Indies.

PLATE 9 : *Waiting for the Nevis Boats (circa 1916)* 17¼ × 21¼. *B. W. Fleck, Esq., Vancouver.*

HORATIO WALKER, R.C.A., N.A. (1858–1938)

Born in Listowel, Ontario. Studied miniature painting in Toronto and in New York. Largely self-taught. Elected R.C.A. in 1918. Member of the National Academy of Design, and the National Institute of Arts and Letters, New York ; The American Water Colour Society ; the Royal Institute of Painters in Water Colours, England. Represented in the Metropolitan Museum of Art, New York, and in various other galleries in the United States, also in public collections of Canada.

PLATE 10 : *Oxen Drinking (1899)* 47½ × 35½. *The National Gallery of Canada, Ottawa.*

PLATE 11 : *The Sugar Bush (1922)* 24 × 18. *R. S. McLaughlin, Esq., Oshawa, Ontario.*

WILLIAM BRYMNER, C.M.G., R.C.A. (1855–1925)

Born in Greenock, Scotland. He was brought by his parents to Canada when still quite young. His father was Dr. Douglas Brymner, the Dominion Archivist. Studied at the Académie Julian in Paris. Principal of the School of the Art Association of Montreal for many years. Elected R.C.A. 1886. Created C.M.G. 1916.

PLATE 12 : *Afterglow (1913)* 29¼ × 35½. *Dr. W. W. Chipman, Montreal.*

MAURICE G. CULLEN, R.C.A. (1877–1934)

Born in St. John's, Newfoundland. Studied first in Montreal, later in Paris from 1889–1895 under Delaunay and Roll. Elected an associate member of the Société Nationale, Paris, 1895 ; returned to Canada in 1896 ; elected to the Royal Canadian Academy, 1907. Served as an official artist for the Canadian War Memorials, 1918.

PLATE 13 : *The Deep Pool (1926)* 24 × 18. *William R. Watson, Esq., Montreal.*

PLATE 14 : *View of Quebec from Levis (1920)* 31½ × 40½. *University Club, Montreal.*

PLATE 15 : *Old Houses, Montreal (1897)* 24 × 34. *Art Association of Montreal.*

PLATE 16 : *Ice Harvest (1908)* 29½ × 39½. *The National Gallery of Canada, Ottawa.*

JAMES WILSON MORRICE, R.C.A. (1865–1924)

Born in Montreal. Studied in Paris at the Académie Julian and later with Henri Harpignies, the French landscape painter. A member of the Société Nationale des Beaux-Arts, the Société Nouvelle, and the Salon d'Automne, Paris ; The International Society, London ; honorary non-resident member of the Royal Canadian Academy. Represented in the Jeu de Paume Museum, Paris ; the Tate Gallery, London ; the Museum of Modern Western Art, Moscow ; and in public galleries at Lyons, France, and Philadelphia, as well as in public collections in Canada.

PLATE 17 : *Entrance to a Quebec Village, Winter (1909)* 23½ × 31½. *Mrs. T. C. Darling, Westmount, Quebec.*

PLATE 18 : *Canadian Square in Winter (circa 1906)* 20 × 22. *A. G. Dawes, Esq., Montreal.*

PLATE 19 : *The Dufferin Terrace, Quebec (1911)* 23¼ × 28¾. *Mount Royal Club, Montreal.*

PLATE 20 : *Bull Ring (1905)* 26 × 32. *Huntly Drummond, Esq., Montreal.*

PLATE 21 : *Sur les Quais (Le Pont Royal) (circa 1904)* 23 × 28. *Miss Sophia Reford, Montreal.*

PLATE 22 : *In a Garden, The West Indies (circa 1921)* 25 × 21. *Huntly Drummond, Esq., Montreal.*

PLATE 23 : *Landscape, North Africa (circa 1920) (oil on wooden panel)* 6 × 8. *David Morrice, Esq., Montreal.*

COLOUR PLATE I : page 9.
" *The Ferry, Quebec* " *(circa 1909)* 23½ × 31½. *The National Gallery of Canada, Ottawa.*

CHARLES W. JEFFERYS, R.C.A. (1869–   )

Born in Rochester, England. Came to Canada in 1881, and settled in Toronto, where he studied art. Later he worked for some years as an illustrator in New York. President of Graphic Arts Club, Toronto, 1903–4. Elected R.C.A. 1926. Worked for the Canadian War Memorials, 1916–1918.

PLATE 24 : *Prairie Trail* (1918) 25½ × 30½.   *The Art Gallery of Toronto.*

CLARENCE A. GAGNON, R.C.A. (1880–1942)

Born in Montreal.   Studied at the Art Association of Montreal under William Brymner, and at the Académie Julian in Paris. Elected R.C.A. 1922.   Represented by etchings in the Petit Palais, Paris ; South Kensington Museum, London ; and in Dresden, Florence, Venice, and The Hague, and by paintings in many Canadian galleries.

PLATE 25 : *Evening on the North Shore* (1916) 29⅝ × 33½. *The National Gallery of Canada, Ottawa.*

PLATE 26 : *Laurentian Village* (1926) 29 × 36.   *Provincial Museum, Quebec.*

PLATE 27 : *Street, Village in the Laurentians* (circa 1920) 21⅝ × 28½. *R. S. McLaughlin, Esq., Oshawa, Ontario.*

JOHN WILLIAM BEATTY, R.C.A. (1868–1941)

Born in Toronto.   Studied first in that city and later at the Académie Julian in Paris.   He was one of the first painters to travel and sketch by canoe in the Canadian northland.   Served as an official artist for the Canadian War Memorials, 1917.   Instructor at the Ontario College of Art for many years.

PLATE 28 : *Beechwood* (circa 1916) 35 × 41.   *Hart House, University of Toronto.*

PLATE 29 : *Morning, Algonquin Park* (1919) 30 × 36. *The National Gallery of Canada, Ottawa.*

JAMES E. H. MACDONALD, R.C.A. (1873–1932)

Born in Durham, England, of Canadian parents.   Came to Canada in 1887.   Studied at the Hamilton Art School and the Central Ontario School of Art, Toronto.   Elected R.C.A. 1931. Principal of the Ontario College of Art, 1928–1932.   A member of the Group of Seven, 1919-1932.   He is represented in public collections in both Canada and the United States.

PLATE 30 : *Tracks and Traffic* (1912) 28 × 40.   *The Art Gallery of Toronto.*

PLATE 31 : *Mist Fantasy* (1922) 21 × 26.   *The Art Gallery of Toronto.*

PLATE 32 : *Gleams on the Hills* (1921) 32 × 34.   *The National Gallery of Canada, Ottawa.*

PLATE 33 : *Fall of the Leaf* (1922) 47½ × 59½ (*also known as Autumn in Algoma*).   *The National Gallery of Canada, Ottawa.*

PLATE 34 : *The Solemn Land* (1921) 48 × 60.   *The National Gallery of Canada, Ottawa.*

PLATE 35 : *Leaves in the Brook* (1919) 21 × 26.   *Dr. Arnold D. Mason, Toronto.*

PLATE 36 : *A Northern Hilltop* (1931) 30 × 35.   *H. S. Southam, Esq., C.M.G., Ottawa.*

PLATE 37 : *Snow in the Mountains* (circa 1930) (*oil on wooden panel*) 8½ × 10½.   *The Art Gallery of Toronto.*

COLOUR PLATE II : page 13.
"*The Potato Field, Ontario, in Summer*" (1920).   *Oil on wooden panel, 8½ × 10½.   The Rt. Hon. Vincent Massey, P.C., London.*

TOM THOMSON (1877–1917)

Born in Claremont, Ontario ; grew up at Leith, near Owen Sound, Ontario.   Largely self tutored, but studied decorative design to some extent.   For eight months each year after 1913 he lived in Algonquin Park, where he painted the Canadian northland. His death came by drowning in July, 1917.

PLATE 38 : *The Pointers* (circa 1915) 40 × 45½ (*also known as Pageant of the North*).   *Hart House, University of Toronto.*

PLATE 39 : *Chill November* (1916) 34¼ × 38¼.   *Women's Conservation Art Association, Sarnia, Ontario.*

PLATE 40 : *Pine Island* (begun 1914, finished 1916) 60¼ × 50. *The National Gallery of Canada, Ottawa.*

PLATE 41 : *Northern River* (1915) 45 × 40.   *The National Gallery of Canada, Ottawa.*

PLATE 42 : *October* (1917) 32 × 34.   *Dr. Frederick MacCallum, Toronto.*

PLATE 43 : *The Jack Pine* (1916) 50¼ × 55.   *The National Gallery of Canada, Ottawa.*

PLATE 44 : *The Waterfall* (1915) 8½ × 10¼ (*oil on wooden panel*). *The National Gallery of Canada, Ottawa.*

PLATE 45 : *Spring Ice* (1916) 27½ × 39¾.   *The National Gallery of Canada, Ottawa.*

PLATE 86 : *Decoration* (circa 1916) 12 × 44.   *Miss Esther Williams, Toronto.*

COLOUR PLATE III : page 17.
"*The Artist's Hut*" (circa 1916).   *Oil on wooden panel, 8½ × 10½. The National Gallery of Canada, Ottawa.*

ALEXANDER YOUNG JACKSON (1883–   )

Born in Montreal.   Studied first at the evening classes of the Council of Arts and Manufactures, Montreal ; later at the Art Institute, Chicago, and at the Académie Julian in Paris.   Elected to the Royal Canadian Academy in 1919 but resigned in 1932. Served as an official artist for the Canadian War Memorials.   Represented in the Tate Gallery, London ; the Art Gallery of Dunedin, New Zealand, and in many Canadian galleries.   A member of the Group of Seven 1919–1933, and the Canadian Group of Painters, 1933.   He now lives in Toronto.

PLATE 46 : *First Snow, Georgian Bay* (1920) 21 × 26.   *J. S. McLean, Esq., Toronto.*

PLATE 47 : *St. Lawrence in Winter* (1921) 21 × 25½.   *F. T. Jenkins, Esq., Montreal.*

PLATE 48 : *Indian Home* (1925) 21 × 26.   *Miss Isobel McLaughlin, Toronto.*

PLATE 49 : *Ruisseau Jureux* (1931) 27 × 32.   *H. S. Southam, Esq., C.M.G., Ottawa.*

PLATE 50 : *Precambrian Hills* (1938) 28 × 26.   *The Art Gallery of Toronto.*

PLATE 51 : *Winter Morning, Charlevoix County* (1933) 25 × 32. *The Art Gallery of Toronto.*

PLATE 52 : *Barns* (1926) 32 × 40.   *The Art Gallery of Toronto.*

PLATE 53 : *Winter in Quebec, St. Urbain* (1933) 25 × 32.   *The Art Gallery of Dunedin, New Zealand.*

COLOUR PLATE IV : page 19.
"*Algoma Lake*" (1938) 25 × 32.   *H. O. McCurry, Esq., Ottawa.*

FRANZ H. JOHNSTON, A.R.C.A. (1888–   )

Born in Toronto.   Studied at the Central Ontario School of Art, Toronto, and at the Pennsylvania Academy of the Fine Arts, Philadelphia.   Worked for the Canadian War Memorials, 1917– 1918.   His paintings were exhibited at the first Group of Seven show in 1920, but he later withdrew from the Group.   Principal, Winnipeg School of Art, 1920–1924.   He now lives in Toronto.

PLATE 54. *Fire Swept, Algoma* (1920) 50¼ × 66.   *The National Gallery of Canada, Ottawa.*

ARTHUR LISMER, A.R.C.A. (1885–   )

Born in Sheffield, England.   Studied first at the Sheffield School of Art, where he was awarded a scholarship ; later, at the Académie Royale des Beaux-Arts, Antwerp.   Came to Canada in 1911.   A member of the Group of Seven, 1919–1933, and the Canadian Group of Painters, 1933.   He was Principal of the Nova Scotia College of Art from its reorganization in 1917 until 1919, and while in Halifax worked for the Canadian War Memorials, 1917–18. Vice-Principal of the Ontario College of Art, 1919–1928.   Educational Supervisor, Art Gallery of Toronto, and Director of the Children's Art Centre from 1928–1938.   Visiting Professor of Fine Arts, Teachers' College, Columbia University, N.Y., 1938– 1939.   He is at present Educational Director, the Art Association of Montreal.

PLATE 55 : *The Guide's Home* (1914) 39½ × 44½.   *The National Gallery of Canada, Ottawa.*

PLATE 56 : *Rocks, Pine and Sunlight* (1920) 21 × 28½.   *The Art Gallery of Toronto.*

PLATE 57 : *September Gale* (1922) 48 × 64. *The National Gallery of Canada, Ottawa.*

PLATE 58 : *Rain in the North Country* (1924) 28½ × 34½. *H. S. Southam, Esq., C.M.G., Ottawa.*

PLATE 85 : *Convoy in Bedford Basin* (1918) 36 × 102. *Canadian War Memorials Collection, Ottawa.*

FRANKLIN CARMICHAEL (1890–   )

Born in Orillia, Ontario. Studied at the Ontario College of Art, Toronto, and the Académie Royale des Beaux-Arts, Antwerp. A member of the Group of Seven, 1919–1933, and the Canadian Group of Painters, 1933 ; elected R.C.A., 1938. Represented in the South African National Gallery, Capetown, and in Canadian galleries. Instructor, Ontario College of Art since 1932.

PLATE 59 : *October Haze (circa 1935)* 38 × 48. *St. Hilda's College, Toronto.*

PLATE 60 : *A Northern Village* (1926) 40 × 48. *Property of the Artist.*

PLATE 74 : *Jackfish Village* (1925) 18½ × 21 *(water colour). The Art Gallery of Toronto.*

LAWREN S. HARRIS (1885–   )

Born in Brantford, Ontario. Studied in Germany and in other European countries; returned definitely to Canada in 1911. Awarded Gold Medal at the Sesquincentennial Exposition, Philadelphia, 1926, and a prize of five hundred dollars at the Baltimore Pan-American Exhibition, 1931. A member of the Group of Seven, 1919–1933, and the Canadian Group of Painters, 1933. He now lives in Vancouver.

PLATE 61 : *January Thaw, Edge of Town* (1923) 42 × 50. *Arts and Letters Club, Toronto.*

PLATE 62 : *Grey Day in Town* (1926) 32¼ × 38½. *H. S. Southam, Esq., C.M.G., Ottawa.*

PLATE 63 : *Lighthouse, Father Point* (1930) 42 × 50. *Property of the Artist.*

PLATE 64 : *Bylot Island* (1931) 42½ × 50. *The National Gallery of Canada, Ottawa.*

PLATE 65 : *Pic Island, Lake Superior* (1928) 48 × 60. *R. S. McLaughlin, Esq., Oshawa, Ontario.*

PLATE 66 : *Country North of Lake Superior* (1927) 48 × 60. *The Art Gallery of Toronto.*

PLATE 67 : *North Shore, Lake Superior* (1926) 40 × 50. *The National Gallery of Canada, Ottawa.*

FREDERICK HORSMAN VARLEY, A.R.C.A. (1881–   )

Born in Sheffield, England. Studied at the School of Art, Sheffield, and L'Académie Royale des Beaux-Arts, Antwerp. Came to Canada in 1912. Served as an official artist for the Canadian War Memorials. Head of Department of Drawing and Painting, School of Decorative and Applied Arts, Vancouver, 1926–1933. A member of the Group of Seven, 1913–1933, and the Canadian Group of Painters, 1933.

PLATE 68 : *Someday the People will Return* (1918) 72 × 90. *Canadian War Memorials Collection, Ottawa.*

PLATE 69. *Georgian Bay (circa 1920)* 52 × 64. *The National Gallery of Canada, Ottawa.*

PLATE 70 : *Gypsy Head (circa 1915)* 24 × 20. *H. Mortimer Lamb, Esq., Vancouver.*

PLATE 71 : *Self Portrait (circa 1920)* 24 × 20. *The National Gallery of Canada, Ottawa.*

PLATE 72 : *John (circa 1920)* 24 × 20. *The National Gallery of Canada, Ottawa.*

PLATE 73 : *Vera (circa 1930)* 24 × 20. *The Right Hon. Vincent Massey, P.C., London, England.*

ALFRED JOSEPH CASSON, R.C.A. (1898–   )

Born in Toronto and studied art in that city. A member of the Group of Seven, 1926–1933, and the Canadian Group of Painters, 1933; elected to the Royal Canadian Academy, 1939.

PLATE 75 : *Approaching Storm, Lake Superior* (1929) *(water colour)* 17 × 20. *The National Gallery of Canada, Ottawa.*

PLATE 76 : *Old House at Parry Sound, Ontario* (1930) 37 × 45. *Office of International Business Machines, Inc., New York.*

PLATE 77 : *Church at Magnetawan* (1930) 37 × 45. *The National Gallery of Canada, Ottawa.*

ALBERT HENRY ROBINSON, R.C.A. (1881–   )

Born in Hamilton, Ontario. Studied first in Hamilton, later went to Paris and studied at the Académie Julian, and at the École des Beaux-Arts. Taught at the Hamilton Art School before moving to Montreal about 1909. Elected R.C.A. 1920. Member of the Canadian Group of Painters, 1933. Worked for the Canadian War Memorials, 1918. Represented in the Musée National du Luxembourg, Paris, and in Canadian galleries.

PLATE 78 : *Church in Westmount* (1920) 22 × 26. *The National Gallery of Canada, Ottawa.*

PLATE 79 : *Returning from Easter Mass* (1922) 27 × 32. *The Art Gallery of Toronto.*

LIONEL LEMOINE FITZGERALD (1890–   )

Born in Winnipeg. Studied at the Keszthelyi School of Art, Winnipeg, and at the Art Students' League, New York. A member of the Group of Seven, 1932–1933, and the Canadian Group of Painters, 1933. Principal, Winnipeg School of Art since 1929.

PLATE 80 : *Doc Snider's House* (1930) 29½ × 33½. *The National Gallery of Canada, Ottawa.*

PLATE 81 : *Williamson's Garage* (1928) 22 × 18. *The National Gallery of Canada, Ottawa.*

PLATE 87 : *Landscape with trees* (1934) *(drawing)* 13½ × 16⅝. *The National Gallery of Canada, Ottawa.*

EDWIN HEADLEY HOLGATE, R.C.A. (1892–   )

Born in Allandale, Ontario. Studied at the Art Association of Montreal under William Brymner, and in Paris under Lucien Simon, Réné Menard, and Adolph Milman. Elected R.C.A. 1935. A member of the Group of Seven, 1931–1933, and the Canadian Group of Painters, 1933. Instructor, Art Association of Montreal, 1935–1940.

PLATE 82 : *The Lumberjack* (1926) 26 × 21½. *Women's Conservation Art Association, Sarnia.*

PLATE 83 : *Interior with Nude* (1934) 30 × 25. *The Art Gallery of Toronto.*

PLATE 84 : *Totem Poles, Gitsegiuklas* (1927) 32 × 32. *The National Gallery of Canada, Ottawa.*

THE PLATES

1. PAUL KANE: PORTRAIT OF KEE-A-KEE-KA-SA-COO-WAY. AFTER 1850.
TORONTO, ROYAL ONTARIO MUSEUM

2. PAUL KANE: INDIAN ENCAMPMENT ALONG THE ISLANDS OF LAKE HURON. PROBABLY 1845.
TORONTO, THE ART GALLERY OF TORONTO

3. CORNELIUS KRIEGHOFF: MONTMORENCY FALLS IN WINTER.   1853.   MONTREAL, COL. GEORGE S. CANTLIE

4. CORNELIUS KRIEGHOFF: MERRYMAKING. 1860. QUEBEC, J. T. ROSS, ESQ.

5. CORNELIUS KRIEGHOFF: THE HUNTERS. 1858. TORONTO, DR. J. L. ROBINSON

6. HOMER R. WATSON: THE LONE CATTLE SHED. 1894. TORONTO, MRS. N. W. ROWELL

7. HOMER R. WATSON: THE FLOOD GATE. 1900. OTTAWA, THE NATIONAL GALLERY OF CANADA

8. AURÈLE DE FOYE SUZOR-CÔTÉ: FRANÇOIS TAILLON. 1921. MONTREAL, ART ASSOCIATION OF MONTREAL

9. FRANKLIN BROWNELL : WAITING FOR THE NEVIS BOATS. c. 1916. VANCOUVER, B. W. FLECK, ESQ.

10. HORATIO WALKER: OXEN DRINKING. 1899. OTTAWA, THE NATIONAL GALLERY OF CANADA

11. HORATIO WALKER: THE SUGAR BUSH. 1922. OSHAWA, ONTARIO, R. S. McLAUGHLIN, ESQ.

12. WILLIAM BRYMNER: AFTERGLOW.   1913.   MONTREAL, DR. W. W. CHIPMAN

13. MAURICE G. CULLEN: THE DEEP POOL. 1926. MONTREAL, WILLIAM R. WATSON, ESQ.

14. MAURICE G. CULLEN: VIEW OF QUEBEC FROM LEVIS. 1920. MONTREAL, THE UNIVERSITY CLUB OF MONTREAL

15. MAURICE G. CULLEN: OLD HOUSES. 1897. MONTREAL, ART ASSOCIATION OF MONTREAL

16. MAURICE G. CULLEN: ICE HARVEST. 1908. OTTAWA, THE NATIONAL GALLERY OF CANADA

17. JAMES WILSON MORRICE: ENTRANCE TO A QUEBEC VILLAGE, WINTER. 1909.
WESTMOUNT, QUEBEC, MRS. T. C. DARLING

18. JAMES WILSON MORRICE: CANADIAN SQUARE IN WINTER.   c. 1906.   MONTREAL, A. G. DAWES, ESQ.

19. JAMES WILSON MORRICE: THE DUFFERIN TERRACE, QUEBEC. 1911. MONTREAL, MOUNT ROYAL CLUB

20. JAMES WILSON MORRICE: THE BULL RING. 1905. MONTREAL, HUNTLY DRUMMOND, ESQ.

21. JAMES WILSON MORRICE: SUR LES QUAIS (LE PONT ROYAL).   c. 1904.   MONTREAL, MISS SOPHIA REFORD

22. JAMES WILSON MORRICE :   IN A GARDEN, THE WEST INDIES.   c. 1921.   MONTREAL, HUNTLY DRUMMOND, ESQ.

23. JAMES WILSON MORRICE: LANDSCAPE, NORTH AFRICA. c. 1920. MONTREAL, DAVID MORRICE, ESQ.

24. CHARLES W. JEFFERYS: PRAIRIE TRAIL. 1918. TORONTO, THE ART GALLERY OF TORONTO

25. CLARENCE A. GAGNON: EVENING ON THE NORTH SHORE. 1916. OTTAWA, THE NATIONAL GALLERY OF CANADA

26. CLARENCE A. GAGNON: LAURENTIAN VILLAGE. 1926. QUEBEC, PROVINCIAL MUSEUM

27. CLARENCE A. GAGNON: STREET, VILLAGE IN THE LAURENTIANS. c. 1920.
OSHAWA, ONTARIO, R. S. McLAUGHLIN, ESQ.

28. JOHN WILLIAM BEATTY: BEECHWOOD. c. 1916. TORONTO, HART HOUSE, UNIVERSITY OF TORONTO

29. JOHN WILLIAM BEATTY: MORNING, ALGONQUIN PARK. 1919. OTTAWA, THE NATIONAL GALLERY OF CANADA

30. J. E. H. MACDONALD: TRACKS AND TRAFFIC. 1912. TORONTO, THE ART GALLERY OF TORONTO

31. J. E. H. MACDONALD: MIST FANTASY. 1922. TORONTO, THE ART GALLERY OF TORONTO

32. J. E. H. MACDONALD: GLEAMS ON THE HILLS. 1921. OTTAWA, THE NATIONAL GALLERY OF CANADA

33. J. E. H. MACDONALD: FALL OF THE LEAF. 1922. OTTAWA, THE NATIONAL GALLERY OF CANADA

34. J. E. H. MACDONALD: THE SOLEMN LAND. 1921. OTTAWA, THE NATIONAL GALLERY OF CANADA

35. J. E. H. MACDONALD: LEAVES IN THE BROOK. 1919. TORONTO, DR. ARNOLD D. MASON

36. J. E. H. MACDONALD: A NORTHERN HILLTOP. 1931. OTTAWA, H. S. SOUTHAM, ESQ., C.M.G.

37. J. E. H. MACDONALD: SNOW IN THE MOUNTAINS. c. 1930. TORONTO, THE ART GALLERY OF TORONTO

38. TOM THOMSON: THE POINTERS. c. 1915. TORONTO, HART HOUSE, UNIVERSITY OF TORONTO

39. TOM THOMSON: CHILL NOVEMBER. 1916. SARNIA, ONTARIO, THE WOMEN'S CONSERVATION ART ASSOCIATION

40. TOM THOMSON: PINE ISLAND. 1914–1916. OTTAWA, THE NATIONAL GALLERY OF CANADA

41. TOM THOMSON: NORTHERN RIVER. 1915. OTTAWA, THE NATIONAL GALLERY OF CANADA

42. TOM THOMSON: OCTOBER. 1917. TORONTO, DR. FREDERICK MacCALLUM

43. TOM THOMSON: THE JACK PINE. 1916. OTTAWA, THE NATIONAL GALLERY OF CANADA.

44. TOM THOMSON: THE WATERFALL. 1915. OTTAWA, THE NATIONAL GALLERY OF CANADA

45. TOM THOMSON: SPRING ICE.   1916.   OTTAWA, THE NATIONAL GALLERY OF CANADA

46. A. Y. JACKSON: FIRST SNOW, GEORGIAN BAY. 1920. TORONTO, J. S. McLEAN, ESQ.

47. A. Y. JACKSON : ST. LAWRENCE IN WINTER. 1921. MONTREAL, F. T. JENKINS, ESQ.

48. A. Y. JACKSON : INDIAN HOME. 1925. TORONTO, MISS ISOBEL McLAUGHLIN

49. A. Y. JACKSON: RUISSEAU JUREUX. 1931. OTTAWA, H. S. SOUTHAM, ESQ., C.M.G.

50. A. Y. JACKSON: PRECAMBRIAN HILLS. 1938. TORONTO, THE ART GALLERY OF TORONTO

51. A. Y. JACKSON: WINTER MORNING, CHARLEVOIX COUNTY. 1933. TORONTO, THE ART GALLERY OF TORONTO

52. A. Y. JACKSON: BARNS. 1926. TORONTO, THE ART GALLERY OF TORONTO

53. A. Y. JACKSON: WINTER IN QUEBEC, ST. URBAIN.   1933.   DUNEDIN, NEW ZEALAND, THE ART GALLERY OF DUNEDIN

54. F. H. JOHNSTON: FIRE SWEPT, ALGOMA. 1920. OTTAWA, THE NATIONAL GALLERY OF CANADA

55. ARTHUR LISMER: THE GUIDE'S HOME. 1914. OTTAWA, THE NATIONAL GALLERY OF CANADA

56. ARTHUR LISMER: ROCKS, PINE AND SUNLIGHT.   1920.   TORONTO, THE ART GALLERY OF TORONTO

57. ARTHUR LISMER: SEPTEMBER GALE. 1922. OTTAWA, THE NATIONAL GALLERY OF CANADA

58. ARTHUR LISMER: RAIN IN THE NORTH COUNTRY. 1924. OTTAWA, H. S. SOUTHAM, ESQ., C.M.G.

59. FRANKLIN CARMICHAEL: OCTOBER HAZE. c. 1935. TORONTO, ST. HILDA'S COLLEGE

60. FRANKLIN CARMICHAEL: A NORTHERN VILLAGE. 1926. IN THE ARTIST'S POSSESSION

61. LAWREN S. HARRIS: JANUARY THAW, EDGE OF TOWN.   1923.   TORONTO, THE ARTS AND LETTERS CLUB

62. LAWREN S. HARRIS: GREY DAY IN TOWN. 1926. OTTAWA, H. S. SOUTHAM, ESQ. C.M.G.

63. LAWREN S. HARRIS: LIGHTHOUSE, FATHER POINT. 1930.   IN THE ARTIST'S POSSESSION

64. LAWREN S. HARRIS: BYLOT ISLAND. 1931. OTTAWA, THE NATIONAL GALLERY OF CANADA

65. LAWREN S. HARRIS: PIC ISLAND, LAKE SUPERIOR. 1928. OSHAWA, ONTARIO, R. S. McLAUGHLIN, ESQ.

66. LAWREN S. HARRIS: COUNTRY NORTH OF LAKE SUPERIOR. 1927. TORONTO, THE ART GALLERY OF TORONTO

67. LAWREN S. HARRIS: NORTH SHORE, LAKE SUPERIOR. 1926. OTTAWA, NATIONAL GALLERY OF CANADA

68. FREDERICK HORSMAN VARLEY: SOMEDAY THE PEOPLE WILL RETURN. 1918.
OTTAWA, CANADIAN WAR MEMORIALS COLLECTION

69. FREDERICK HORSMAN VARLEY: GEORGIAN BAY. c. 1920. OTTAWA, THE NATIONAL GALLERY OF CANADA

70. FREDERICK HORSMAN VARLEY: GIPSY HEAD.   c. 1915.   VANCOUVER, H. MORTIMER LAMB, ESQ.

71. FREDERICK HORSMAN VARLEY: SELF PORTRAIT. c. 1920.
OTTAWA, THE NATIONAL GALLERY OF CANADA

72. FREDERICK HORSMAN VARLEY: JOHN. c. 1920. OTTAWA, THE NATIONAL GALLERY OF CANADA

73. FREDERICK HORSMAN VARLEY: VERA. c. 1930. LONDON, THE RIGHT HON. VINCENT MASSEY, P.C.

74. FRANKLIN CARMICHAEL: JACKFISH VILLAGE. 1925. WATERCOLOUR.
TORONTO, THE ART GALLERY OF TORONTO

75. ALFRED J. CASSON: APPROACHING STORM, LAKE SUPERIOR. 1929. WATERCOLOUR.
OTTAWA, THE NATIONAL GALLERY OF CANADA

76. ALFRED J. CASSON: OLD HOUSE AT PARRY SOUND, ONTARIO.   1930.
NEW YORK, OFFICE OF THE INTERNATIONAL BUSINESS MACHINES, INC.

77. ALFRED J. CASSON: CHURCH AT MAGNETAWAN.   1930.   OTTAWA, THE NATIONAL GALLERY OF CANADA

78. ALBERT H. ROBINSON: A CHURCH IN WESTMOUNT. 1920. OTTAWA, THE NATIONAL GALLERY OF CANADA

79. ALBERT H. ROBINSON: RETURNING FROM EASTER MASS.   1922.   TORONTO, THE ART GALLERY OF TORONTO

80. LIONEL LEMOINE FITZGERALD: DOC SNIDER'S HOUSE. 1930. OTTAWA, THE NATIONAL GALLERY OF CANADA

81. LIONEL LEMOINE FITZGERALD: WILLIAMSON'S GARAGE. 1928.
OTTAWA, THE NATIONAL GALLERY OF CANADA

82. EDWIN HEADLEY HOLGATE: THE LUMBERJACK. 1926.
SARNIA, THE WOMEN'S CONSERVATION ART ASSOCIATION

83. EDWIN HEADLEY HOLGATE: INTERIOR WITH NUDE. 1934.
TORONTO, THE ART GALLERY OF TORONTO

84. EDWIN HEADLEY HOLGATE: TOTEM POLES, GITSEGIUKLAS. 1927.
OTTAWA, THE NATIONAL GALLERY OF CANADA

INDEX OF ARTISTS AND COLLECTIONS

INDEX OF ARTISTS

85. ARTHUR LISMER: CONVOY IN BEDFORD BASIN. 1918. OTTAWA, CANADIAN WAR MEMORIALS COLLECTION

INDEX OF COLLECTIONS

86. TOM THOMSON : DECORATION. c. 1916. TORONTO, MISS ESTHER WILLIAMS

87. LIONEL LEMOINE FITZGERALD: LANDSCAPE WITH TREES. 1934.
DRAWING. OTTAWA, THE NATIONAL GALLERY OF CANADA